Yosemite National Park

Animals & Attractions

Billy Grinslott & Kinsey Marie Books

ISBN - 9781960612908

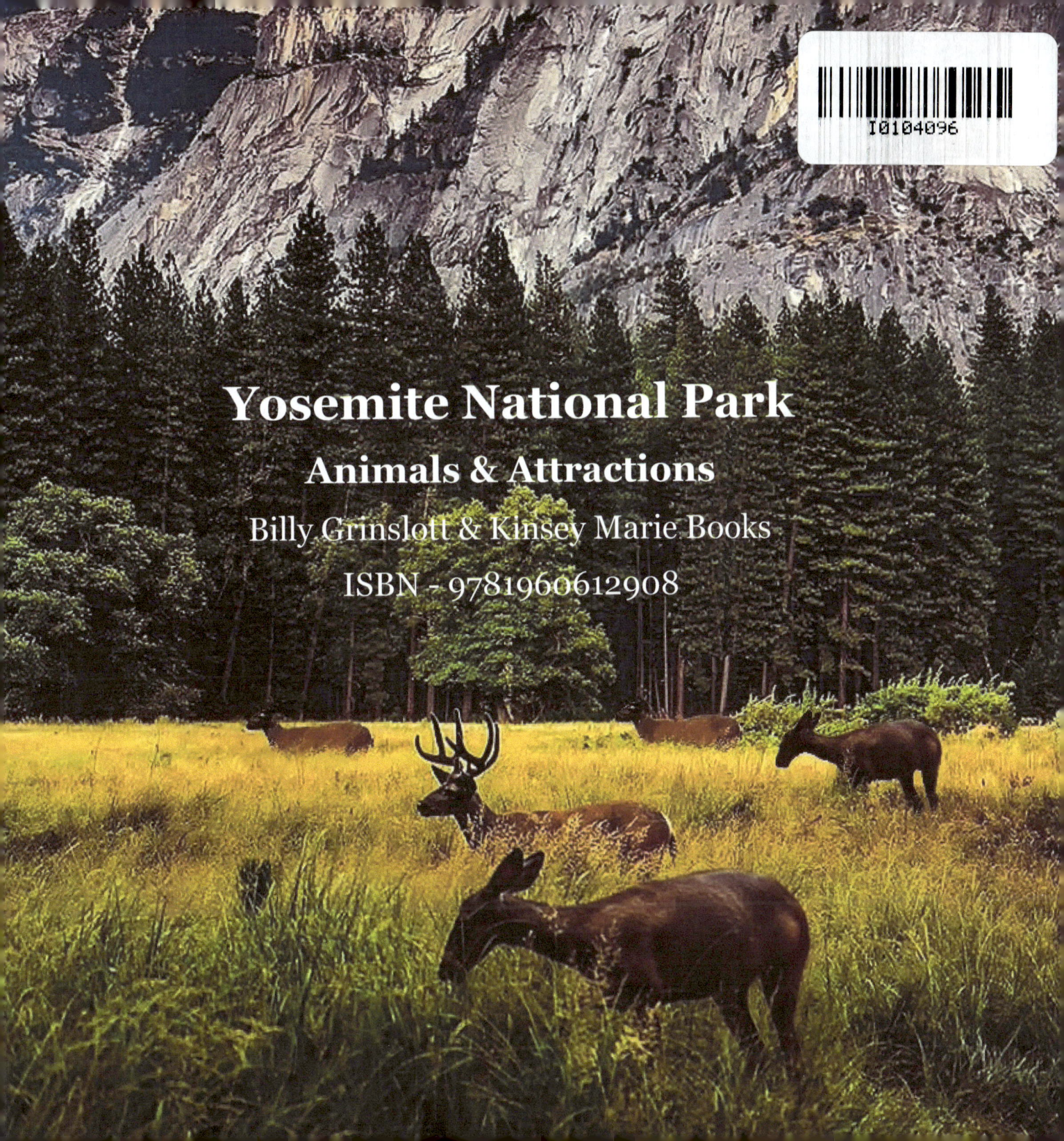

Chipmunks - golden-mantled ground squirrel. Chipmunks are found in many areas. Chipmunks are small members of the squirrel family. They like to eat nuts and seeds. They have pouches inside of their cheeks so they can carry food. They are very friendly and will take food from your hand.

There are many squirrels in the wild. You may see a red or gray squirrel. The most popular is the gray squirrel. You may see a California ground squirrel, or a Douglas squirrel. Squirrels are very acrobatic and can climb trees. Their favorite food is acorns. They like to collect acorns and eat them later.

Flying Squirrels don't fly like birds. They don't have wings. They have skin that is attached to their legs. When they jump from a tree, they spread their legs out and glide through the air. Most glides are 30 feet from tree to tree. But they can glide up to 150 feet.

Though the pika looks more like a mouse, it's related to the rabbit. Pikas live in colonies, with other pikas. When they sense danger, they will let out a shrill whistle to let other pikas know that there is danger. Unlike other mammals, pikas don't hibernate in the winter.

This is a Gopher. Gophers are little excavators. They have sharp claws and make tunnels and burrows underground. That's where they live most of the time.

Marmots can't see very far. They are most active during the day because of their poor eyesight. They like to come out of their dens in the morning and afternoon. Marmots have rough fur, small ears, and short tails. Their strong feet and claws are built for digging holes in the dirt. They are nicknamed the whistle pig, for the high-pitched chirp they make to warn other group members of potential Danger.

Weasels are the smallest members of the meat-eating animals. Although small, they do not hibernate and are active all winter. Weasels have long whiskers like cats, to help them feel things. They even have long whiskers on their elbows. When a weasel gets annoyed, it stomps its feet, just like humans do. Weasels are quick, agile, and alert animals. They are excellent climbers and swimmers.

Fishers are native to North America. They hiss and growl when upset. They are closely related to badgers, mink, and otters. Fisher young are known as kits. Fishers are one of the few animals that eat porcupines. Fishers are also called pekan, pequam, wejack, and woolang.

Martens can be distinguished from fishers, because martens are smaller, have orange on their throats and chests, and have pointier ears and snouts. Martens are part of the weasel family. They are very rare and hard to find. Their tail is long, about two thirds of their body size. There are 13 subspecies of American marten that are native to North America.

There are a couple different kinds of skunks in Yosemite the normal and the spotted. Skunks are usually fairly calm as long as you don't frighten them or make sudden movements. If you scare them, they will flip their tail at you and spray you with a stinky potion. It smells really bad when they do spray you. It's Best to keep your distance if you see one.

Badgers live underground with other family members. Badgers are very social and live in groups. A badger den or sett can be centuries old and are used by many generations of badgers. They are very territorial and will protect their area. It's best to stay away from them.

Ringtails look like a racoon. They have stripes on their tails, but their face more resembles a cat. They are a member of the racoon family. Ringtails can be found in some parts of the redwood forest. Ringtails are excellent climbers capable of ascending vertical walls, trees, rocky cliffs and even cactus. They are mostly nocturnal.

Raccoons like to come out at night. Their eyes are made so they can see in the dark. They are called masked bandits because they have a dark mask around their eyes, and they like to raid and eat out of trash cans at night.

Otters have the thickest fur of any animal. The otter is one of the few mammals that use tools, like rocks. A group of sea otters resting together is called a raft.

Otters primarily rely on their sense of touch, whiskers, and forepaws, in murky waters to locate food. Otters have built in pouches of loose skin under their forearms to stash extra food when diving.

Beavers use their teeth to cut and knock down trees. They build dams with them to block water, so they have a place to live and swim. They also eat wood. Beavers can stay underwater for about 8 minutes. Beavers slap their tails on the water to indicate danger. Beavers are the largest rodents in North America.

There are several types of foxes in North America. This is a red fox. Females are called vixens. Red foxes have supersonic hearing. When afraid, red foxes grin or look like they are smiling. Red foxes front paws have five toes, while their hind feet only have four. There are red and gray foxes in Yosemite mountain national park.

The coyote is bigger than a fox. Eastern coyotes are part wolf. Coyotes are great for pest control. They like to eat mice and rats. They can adapt and live almost anywhere, even in the city. They have a yip type of call when they communicate with each other. Coyotes are found in all the United States, except Hawaii.

Bobcats are frequently misidentified as a lynx. Bobcats are part of the lynx family, but they are smaller than a lynx with different markings.

Mule deer get their name because of their mule like ears. Male deer are called bucks and females are does. Males grow new antlers every year. They can run 30 miles per hour. They are bigger than whitetail deer and prefer living in the mountain areas.

The bighorn sheep is part of the sheep family and likes to live in mountainous areas. Females are called ewes and males are called rams. They are called rams because they like to use their horns to slam into things. Their horn size is a symbol of how high they rank in the herd. The bigger their horns are, the higher they rank.

The mountain lion is one of the biggest cats in North America. The largest mountain lion ever recorded weighed 276 pounds. Mountain lions don't roar like other big cats they communicate in different ways, such as chirping, growling, shrieking, and even purring. Mountain Lions are also known as cougars.

Black bears are the smallest members of the bear family. Black Bears love to eat sweet things like berries, fruits, and vegetables. They are good climbers and fast runners. They usually sleep for long periods of time and hibernate during the winter. They typically try to stay away from people. The black bears in Yosemite can have brownish color fur.

Tunnel view leads park visitors to an unforgettable view of Yosemite Valley. Where you can view some of the other attractions. To the left is the sheer 3,000-foot face of El Capitan. To the right is Bridal Veil Fall, spilling from the cliff side into the pine tree valley below it. In the center, in the background at the far end of Yosemite Valley is another park icon, Half Dome. To view this you can drive directly to the parking lot. It is called tunnel view because you drive through a tunnel to get to the parking lot.

Glacier Point is a overlook with an awesome view of Yosemite Valley, Half Dome, and the High Sierra. It is located 30 miles from Yosemite Valley. The Glacier Point Road is open to cars approximately late May through October or November, depending on conditions. You can drive right up to the parking lot for the overview point.

Located in the southern portion of Yosemite is the Mariposa Grove of Giant Sequoias. It is the largest sequoia grove in Yosemite and is home to over 500 mature giant sequoias. A free shuttle provides service from the Mariposa Grove Welcome Plaza, near South Entrance, to the Mariposa Grove. The welcome plaza has about 300 parking spaces and may fill up by late morning.

You can see Yosemite Falls from numerous places around Yosemite Valley. Especially around Yosemite Village and Yosemite Valley Lodge. A one-mile loop trail leads to the base of Yosemite Fall. Alternatively, you can view it from across Yosemite Valley near Leidig Meadow, or while hiking the Upper Yosemite Fall Trail.

Rising nearly 5,000 feet above Yosemite Valley and 8,800 feet above sea level, Half Dome is a Yosemite icon and a great challenge to many hikers. It is a 15-mile hike roundtrip and is not recommended for beginners. As it is a strenuous hike that gains 5 thousand feet in height. Along the way, you'll see outstanding views of Vernal and Nevada Falls, Liberty Cap, Half Dome, and from the shoulder and summit-panoramic views of Yosemite Valley and the High Sierra.

El Capitan is Yosemite's majestic icon known for its sheer cliff face and stunning views. The most convenient place to take pictures is from the El Capitan Picnic Area. You can drive into the picnic area and view it from there. It is located right off Northside Drive.

The Mist Trail is the most used and straightforward route to Vernal Falls. It was named the Mist Trail because it brings you right to the foot of the Vernal falls. So close that you can feel the spray on your face and witness the raw power of this water flowing down the mountain. It is about a 1.5-mile hike to Vernal Fall.

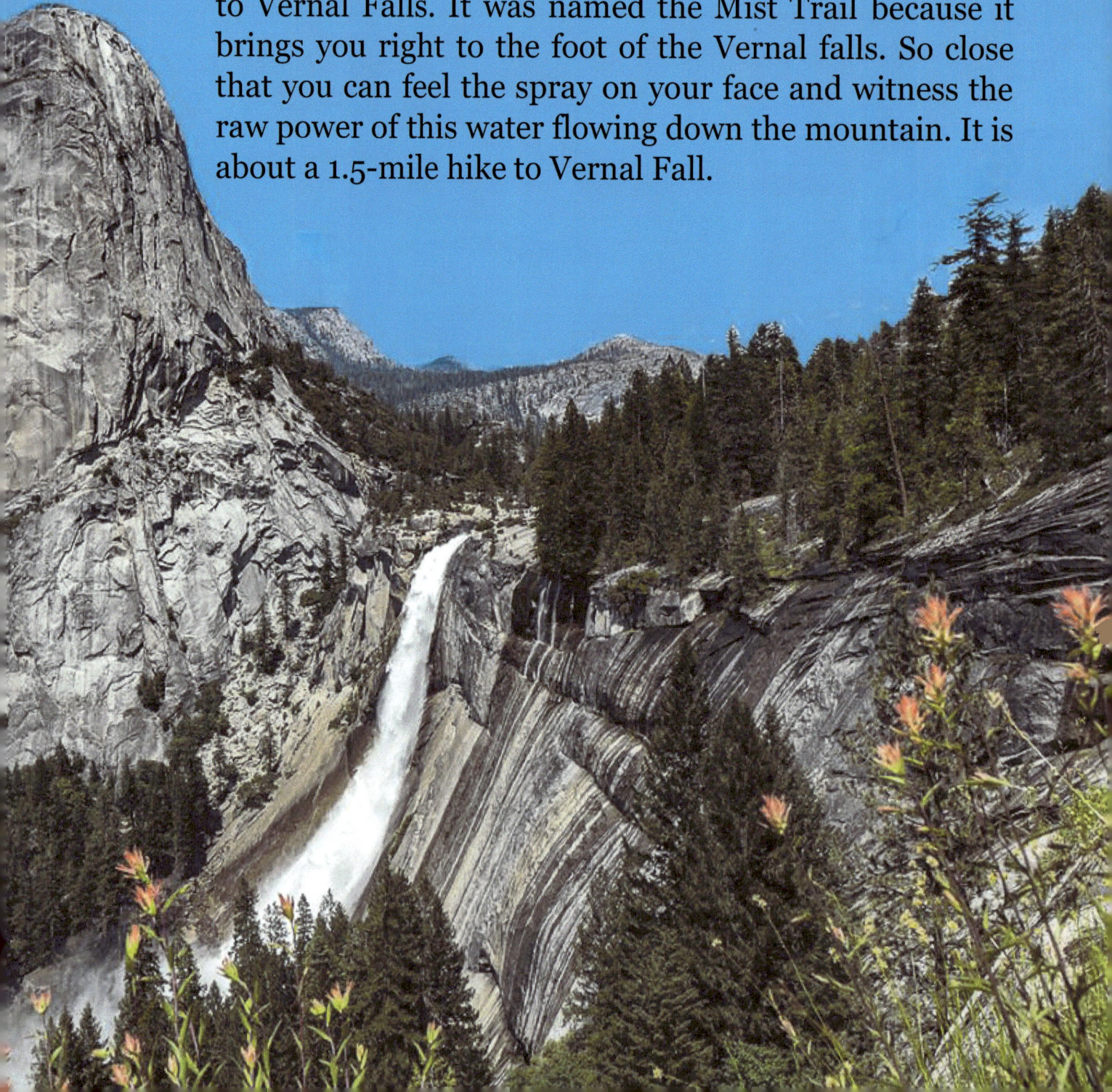

Why stop at Vernal Falls. Hikers can reach the top of Nevada Fall by continuing 1.3-mile hike along the Mist Trail from Vernal Fall. Nevada Fall is a 594-foot-high waterfall. The total loop or roundtrip to visit Vernal Falls and Nevada Fall is around 6.5 miles.

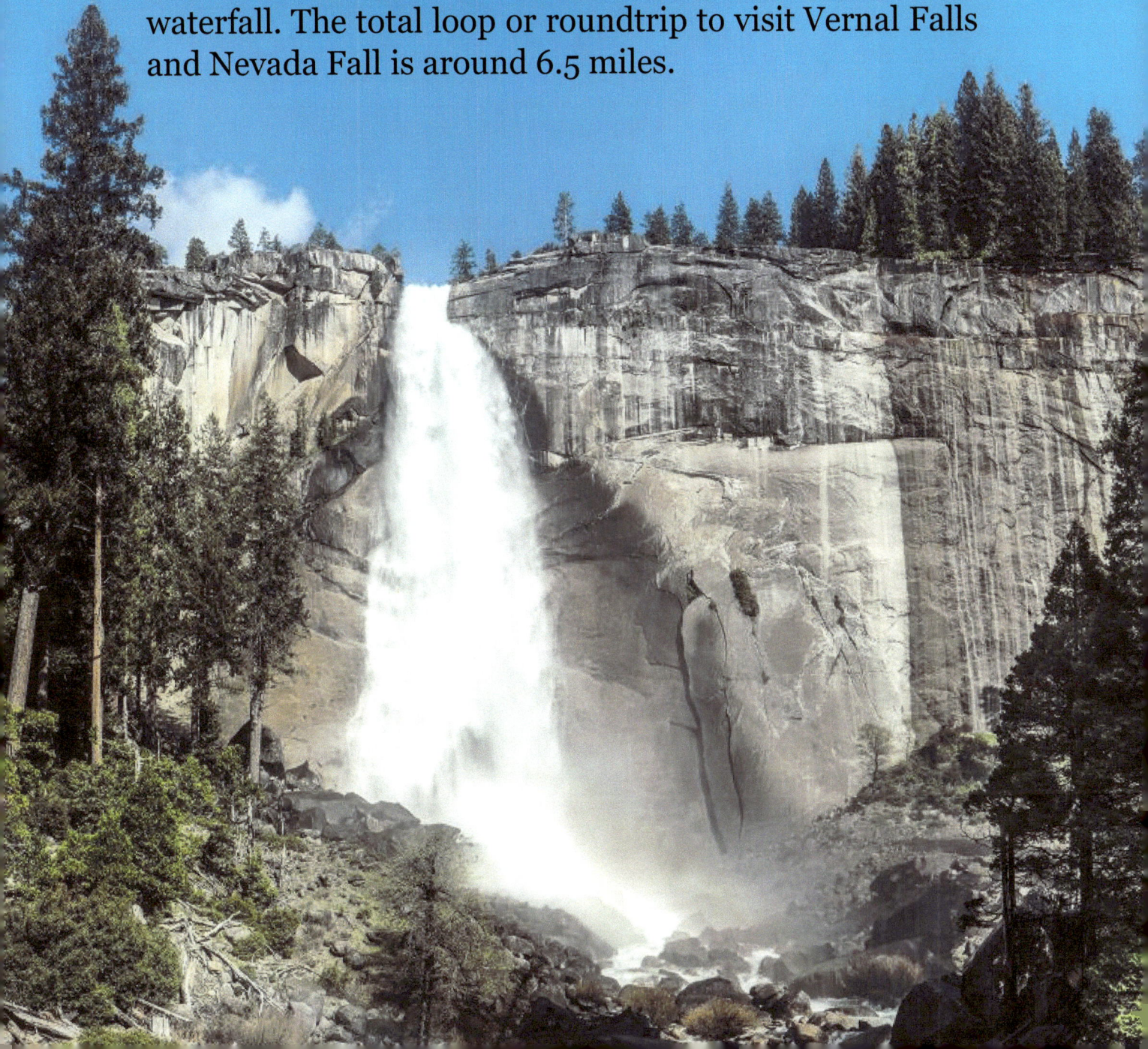

Sentinel Dome. Explore this 2.2-mile roundtrip trail near Yosemite Valley. This wide trail leads mostly across open granite with little shade. Hike up Sentinel Dome's granite slope to enjoy a breathtaking 360-degree view of the park. The trail is mostly easy. It requires little effort until the final stretch up the dome itself, which is short but steep.

Every spring, both visitors and locals look forward to the opening of the Tioga Road, a high-elevation pass that crosses Yosemite National Park. You can see many sights by driving this road. It takes about 2 hours to drive. You will have to pay for a pass to use it. If you're not stopping inside the park and just want to get across the mountains without paying to do it, try Sonora Pass on CA Hwy 108 instead.

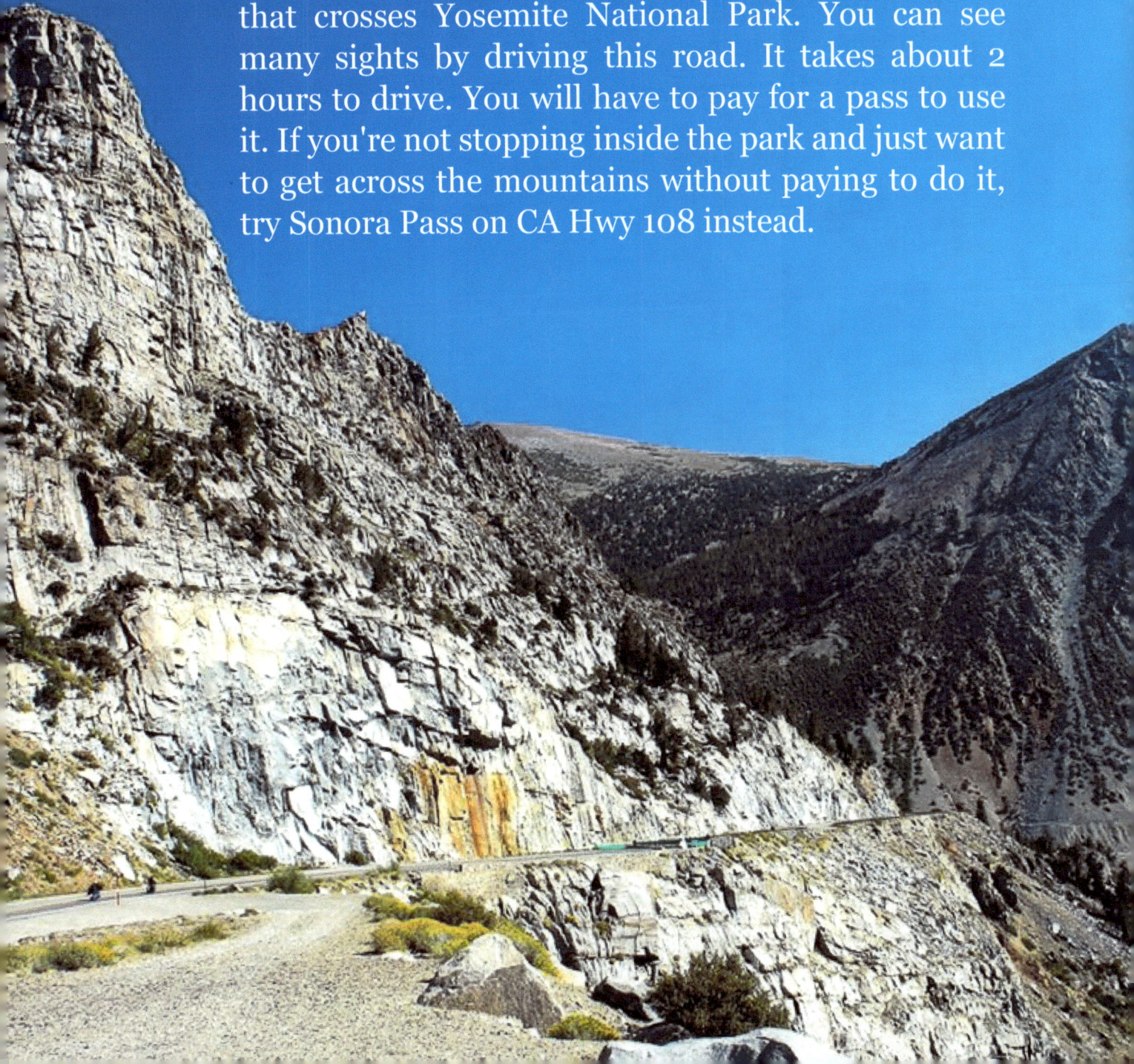

One of the largest high-elevation meadows in the Sierra Nevada, Tuolumne Meadows at 8,600 feet is a popular area that offers scenic views and hiking opportunities. The Tuolumne Meadows Visitor and Wilderness Center. The Tuolumne Meadows Lodge, a store, and campground.

The Taft Point trail is a 2.2-mile roundtrip hike from the Glacier Point Road to a sheer and spectacular overlook of Yosemite Valley. The trail to Taft Point is just another walk in the woods, but you'll never forget Taft Point itself. You can walk, if you dare, right up to the cliff's edge and peer straight down. Not recommended for people who fear heights.

Plunging 620 feet, Bridalveil Fall is the first waterfall you'll see when entering Yosemite Valley. In spring, it thunders. During the rest of the year, look for its light, swaying flow. A paved trail from Yosemite Valley leads from the parking area to the base of this waterfall, which flows year-round.

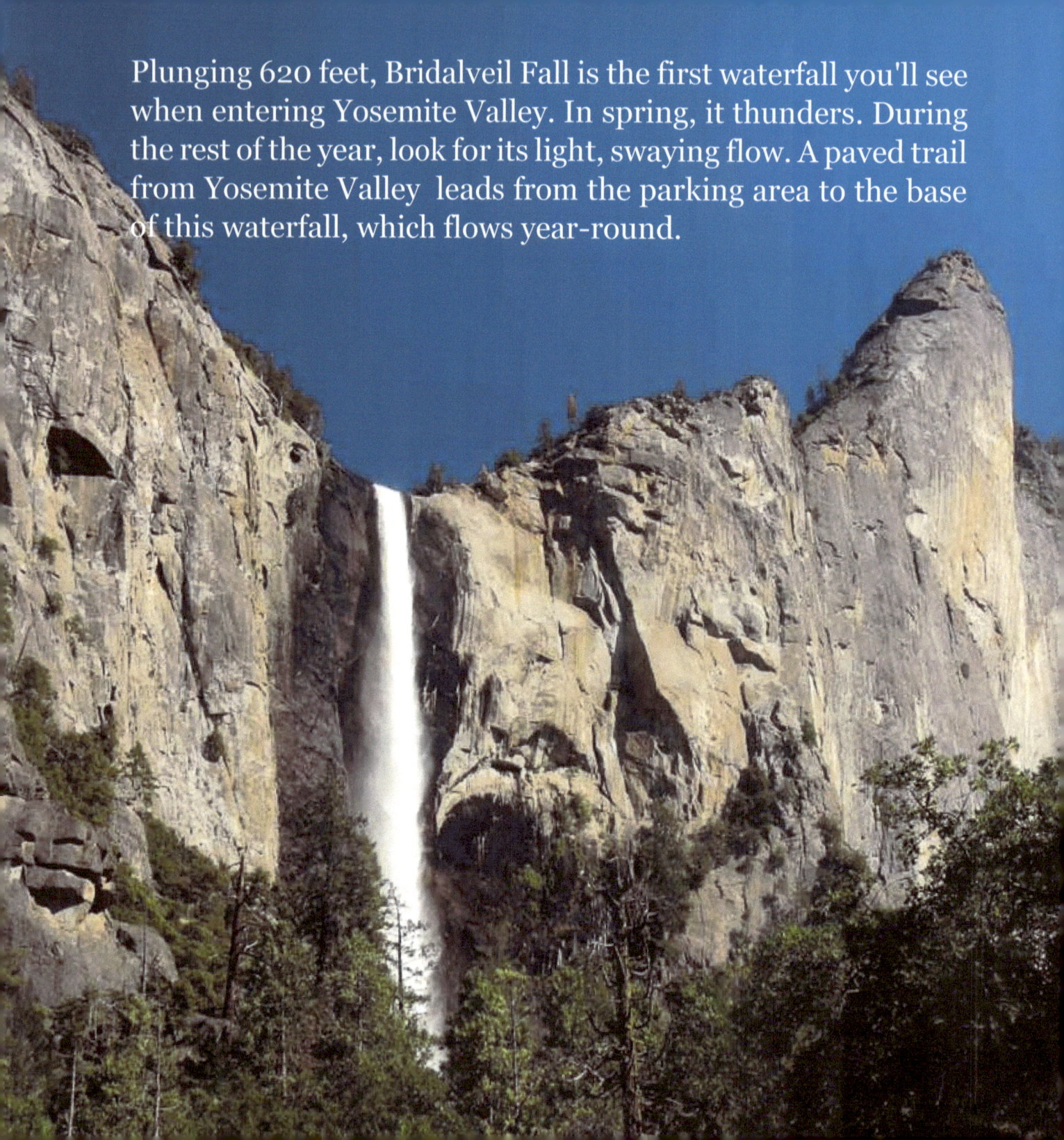

Four Mile Trail. This trail begins near the base of Sentinel Rock and climbs to the top of Yosemite Valley at Glacier Point. The trail has a continuous steep grade. It has spectacular views of Yosemite Valley, El Capitan, Yosemite Falls, and, eventually Half Dome. If you are willing to tackle this strenuous trail, the views are worth it. It is about a 10 mile roundtrip hike.

Hetch Hetchy Valley Lake is a treasure worth visiting in all seasons. In spring, two of North America's tallest waterfalls plummet spectacularly over granite cliffs. Hikers can travel along the Hetch Hetchy reservoir past scenic waterfalls, or access some of Yosemite's stunning wilderness. The trails are different lengths and go in different directions. You will just have to pick one that fits your needs.

Tenaya Lake has remarkable scenery and crystal blue water. It is located off Tioga Road. Tenaya Lake is one of the most popular destinations for summer visitors in Yosemite. It is popular for canoeing and has a picnic area. It's also a popular place for swimming: Just take an easy hike to the shoreline from the picnic area and other areas.

Panorama Trail is Yosemite's most scenic trail. For a moderate hike, start at Glacier Point and hike down to the Valley Floor. Along the way you will walk past two of the famous waterfalls in the park and visit other lookouts. You need to have two cars or take the shuttle bus to the top and walk back down to Yosemite Valley. Although the Panorama Trail is just 8.5 miles in length, it often takes 4-6 hours to complete the trail one way.

Mirror Lake Meadow Trail is an easy to moderate trail to hike. Its 2 miles round trip to lake and back. There is a 5-mile trail that goes around the lake if you decide to hike that after you get to the lake. There are great views of many of the other peaks and sights in the park on this hike.

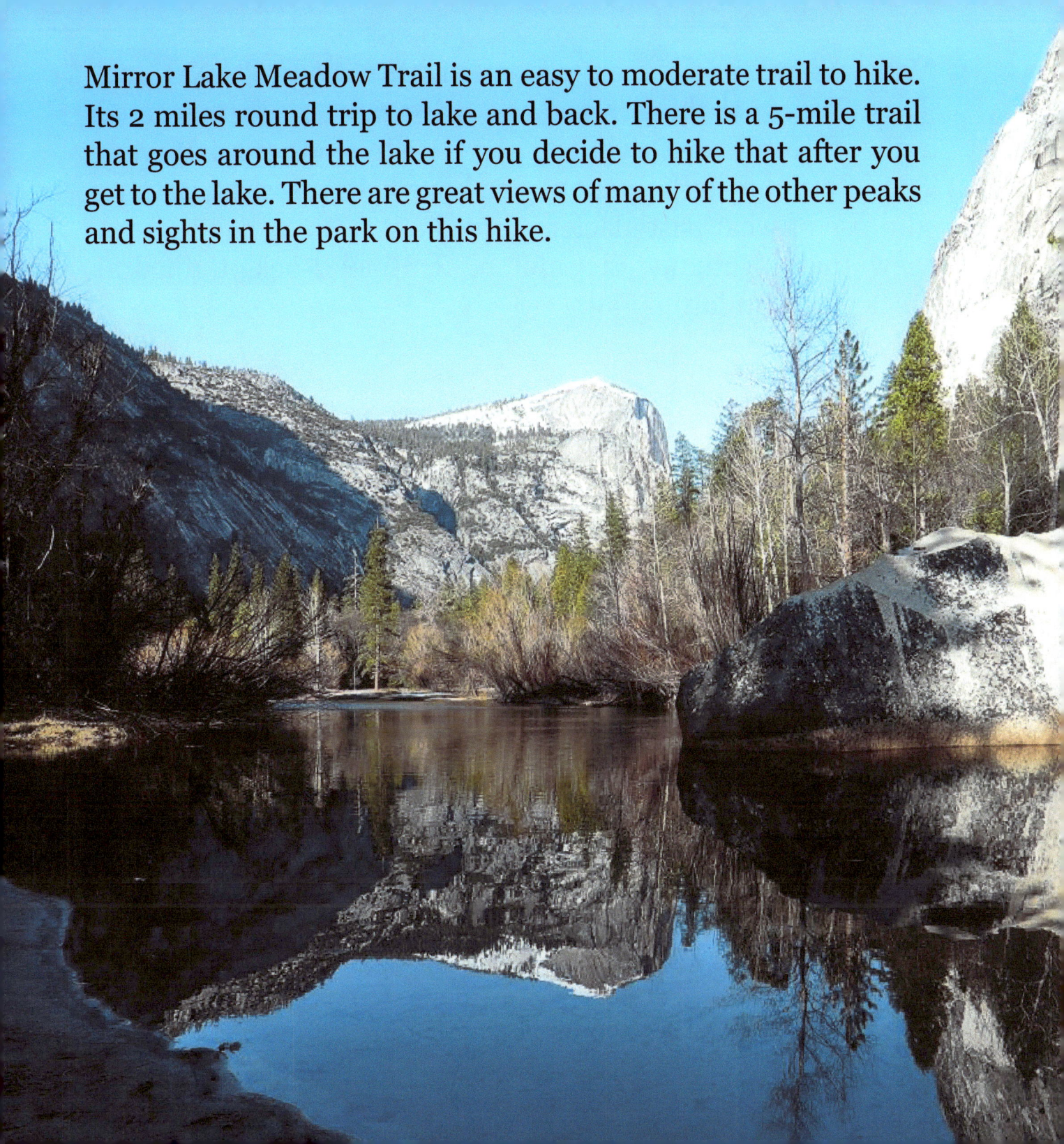

Valley View is one of the top iconic sights at Yosemite National Park. The great thing is you can drive right to it. Its located right off Northside Drive. The best time to photograph there is late afternoon starting about one hour before sunset. Catch a glimpse of what past glaciers carved out from Valley View. A view that highlights El Capitan, Sentinel Rock, Cathedral Rocks, and Bridalveil Fall.

Olmsted Point looks down on Yosemite Valley from the east. Olmsted Point is just off Tioga Road and is one of Yosemite's lowest-effort hikes. Looking west, you'll see a closeup view of Clouds Rest, with Half Dome beyond. Looking east, you'll see the granite domes that envelop Tenaya Lake.

The Merced Grove is home to approximately 20 mature giant sequoias, accessible only on foot. This trail follows an old road that curves down into the Merced Grove, the smallest and most secluded of Yosemite's three sequoia groves. The trail drops down 1.5 miles, making this a moderate hike on the uphill portion

Tuolumne Grove of Giant Sequoias, stop and get your picture taken while standing inside a tree. That's right, that is a base of a tree cut out. Tuolumne Grove trail, a 2.5-mile round-trip hike from the Tioga Road to a grove containing around two dozen mature sequoias.

Clouds Rest is a 10 mile one way, 20 mile roundtrip hike from the valley floor. From Clouds rest you'll have awesome views in every direction, perhaps most gripping of all is straight down. Turn a complete circle and you'll be able to see many of Yosemite landmarks, including Tenaya Lake, Half Dome, Mt. Hoffman, Sentinel Dome, North Dome, and bits of Cathedral Rocks and El Capitan, plus Merced Lake and dozens of other peaks . If you can handle a long hike, its worth it.

Lembert Dome is a short hike about 3.8 miles roundtrip with a big reward. The trail rises steeply for .75 mile to a signed junction. Turn at the sign to reach the top of Lembert Dome. It has spectacular views of Tuolumne Meadows, the Cathedral Range, and surrounding peaks. This loop trail is near Lee Vining, California. Generally considered a moderately challenging route, it takes an average of 2 hours to complete.

Spend a day, or a night, at this stunning alpine lake that reflects an awesome view of Mt. Hoffmann. A short trail leads through a conifer forest and across granite slabs to reach May Lake. Enjoy views of Half Dome and surrounding mountains. Accessible only while Tioga Road is open. Best to check with the park before going.

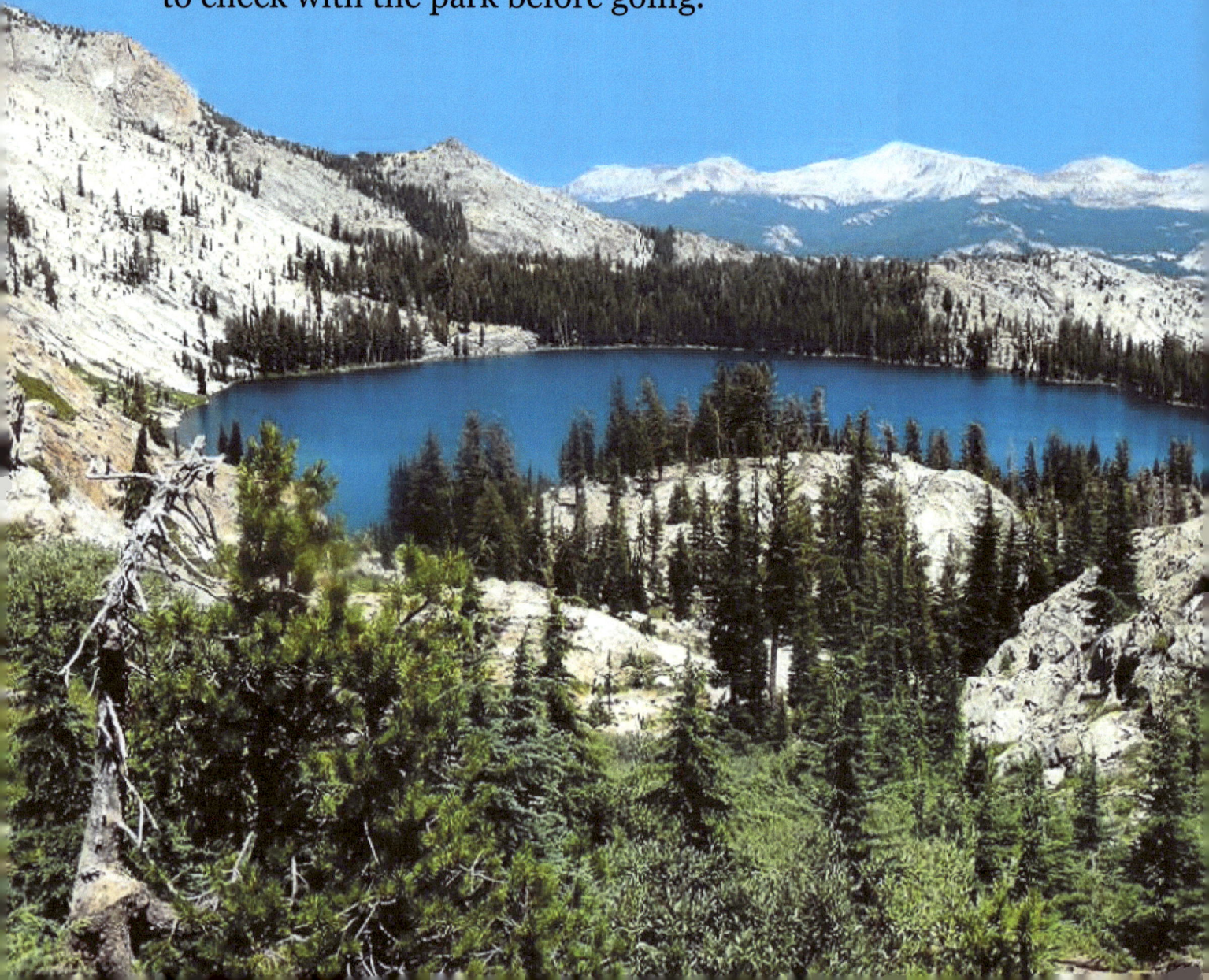

Yosemite Valley Loop Trail offers a rare opportunity to hike on a fairly level trail. While some of the trail passes near roads, much of it takes you through meadows, to talus slopes, the base of granite cliffs, and the Merced River. The length of this trail is a loop of 20 miles. The great thing is you don't have to hike the whole loop, you can turn around at any point. It has awesome views looking up at all mountains, cliffs, waterfalls etc.

Washburn Point. Enjoy this beautiful overlook that provides views of Half Dome and the eastern crest of the Sierra Nevada. From this viewpoint, visitors can take in the view of Vernal and Nevada Falls, and the Sierra crest. This viewpoint can be accessed by car and is located along the Glacier Point Road. There is also Washburn trail if you feel like hiking.

Wapama Falls Trail. Discover this 4.7-mile out-and-back trail near Yosemite Valley. Generally considered a moderately challenging route, it takes an average of 3 hours to complete. Wapama Fall hike follows the shoreline of the reservoir with moderate up and downhill hiking.

Chilnualna Falls is a strenuous hike, but well worth it for its views of the falls and Wawona Dome. Chilnualna Falls are comprised of five large cascades sliding through and over large granite formations above the Wawona basin. The hike is 8.2 miles round trip, 6 hours to complete.

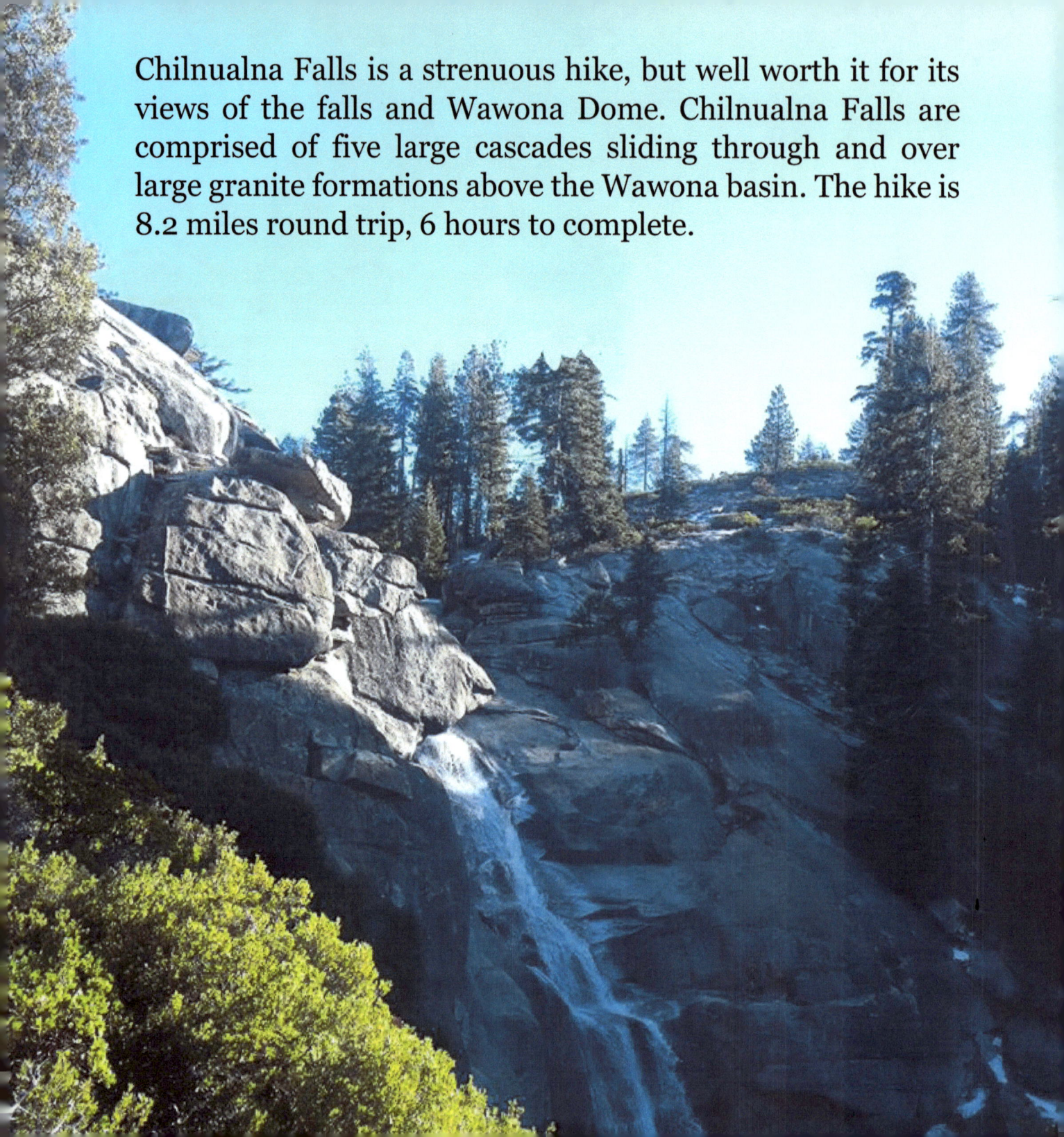

Gaylor Lake, this hike offers some of the most spectacular high-country views off Tioga Road. From the trailhead, climb to a ridge with views of the high Sierra including Mt. Dana and Dana Meadows with its scattered ponds. At the ridge crest, the trail drops 200 feet to Middle Gaylor Lake. Return via the same route. The hike is 2 miles round-trip.

Pothole Dome has magnificent views of Tuolumne Meadows most iconic peaks, domes, and meadows. A trail along the western edge of the meadow curves around to the east side of Pothole Dome. You can climb it for exciting panoramic views. The trail located along Tioga Road, a mile west of the Tuolumne meadows visitor center. Hiking distance is 2.5 miles round trip.

Elizabeth Lake is a 5-mile roundtrip. The hike starts from the Tuolumne meadows campground. It's a moderate hike. 3/4 of the hike is steep uphill. The last part is the most beautiful and the views are spectacular. The lake has different entrances and depends on where you want to stop and spend some time. A great place for a picnic.

Badger Pass Ski Area. You will find groomed trails perfect for cross country skiers, chairlifts that take Alpine skiers to the top of the runs in minutes, a challenging terrain park for snowboarders and skiers to test their limits, and a tubing area where the whole family can experience the thrills together. Badger is also ideal for first time and learning skiers and snowboarders. The starter rental packages include lift tickets and lessons and are very affordable, typically half of the price of major resorts.

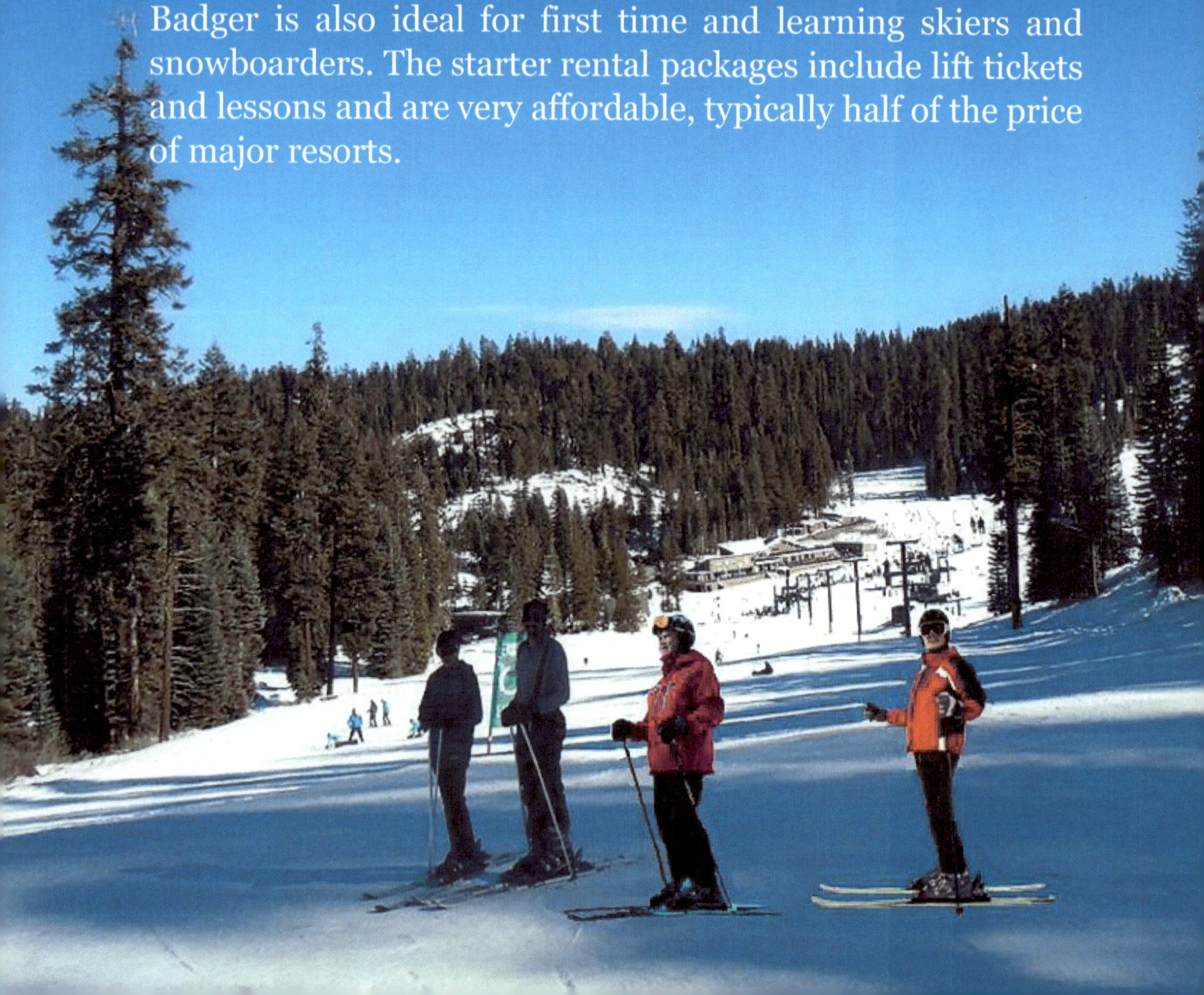

Yosemite Valley Biking. Looking to explore Yosemite with a bicycle? There are over 12 miles of paved bike paths available in Yosemite Valley. You can bring your own bike or rent one for the day. Good way to see the park.

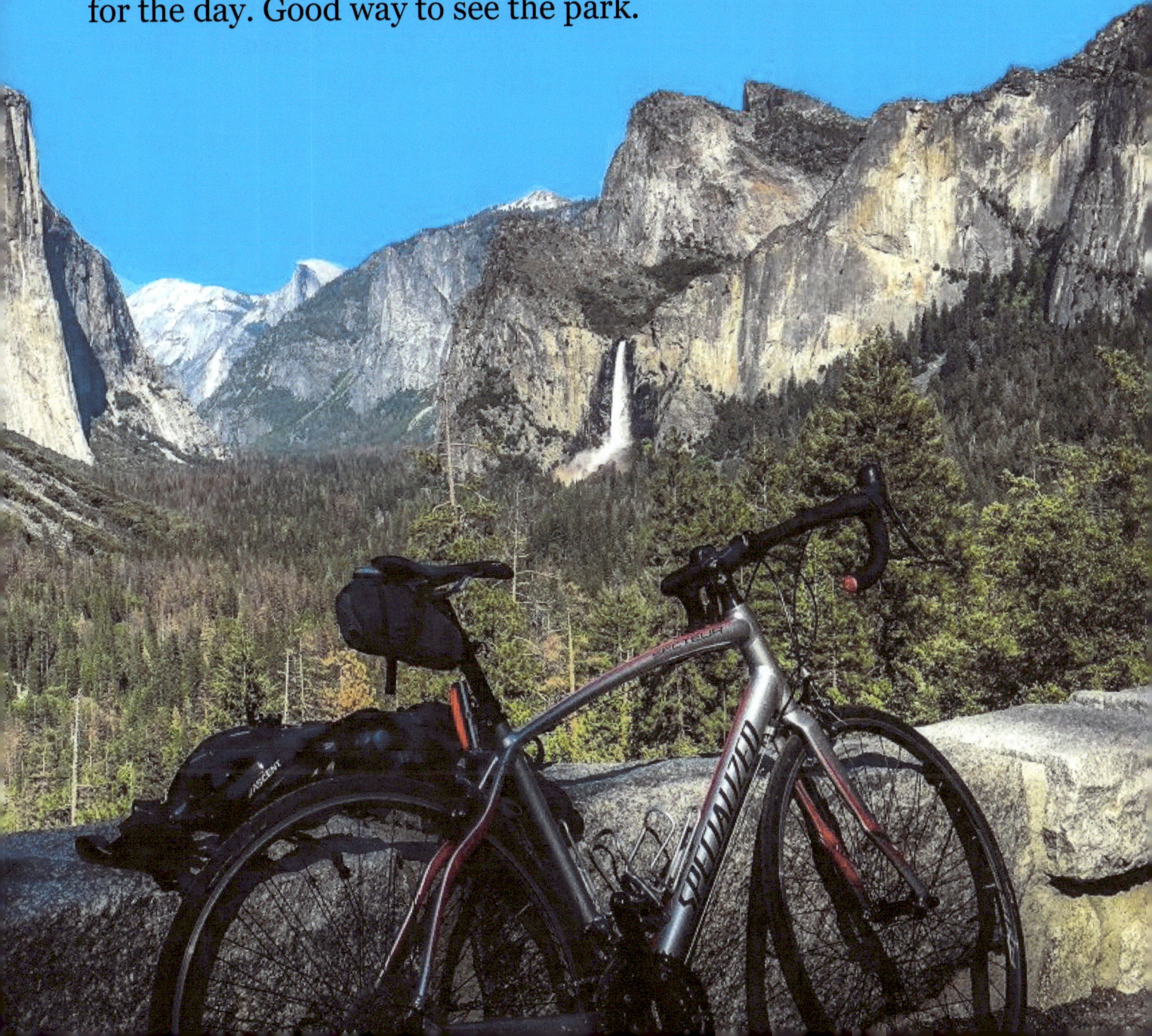

Swinging Bridge Picnic area. Experience a view like none other while standing on the Bridge. Picnic tables and grills are conveniently located at this scenic spot along the Merced River that offers views of the Yosemite Falls and you can swim. Swinging Bridge Picnic Area, is located on Southside Drive, several miles east of Bridalveil Fall.

Cathedral Beach Picnic Area. Located in Yosemite Valley, picnic tables and grills are conveniently located at this scenic spot along the Merced River that offers views of El Capitan. Cathedral Beach Picnic Area is located on Southside Drive, a few miles east of Bridalveil Fall. This area is also accessible via the free Yosemite Valley Shuttle.

Besides all the sights to see in Yosemite. The park offers many other tourist attractions, visitor centers and even hotels to rent. Here's a list of some of the popular ones.

The Valley Visitor Center is located in Yosemite Valley and is the largest in terms of displays, books, postcards and maps. Many trails can be accessed from Yosemite Valley. It's a great place to start.

The Ansel Adams Gallery, located in Yosemite Valley, between the Visitor Center and Post Office, with incredible views of Yosemite Falls, Half Dome, and Glacier Point.

Lamplighters Adventuring Society. Backpacking trips in Yosemite. Your guide brings the meals, gear, and knowledge. You enjoy the adventure of a lifetime. Easy way to hike and backpack.

Yosemite Museum Gallery. Pioneer Yosemite History Center. Nature Center at Happy Isles. Yosemite Conservation Heritage Center.

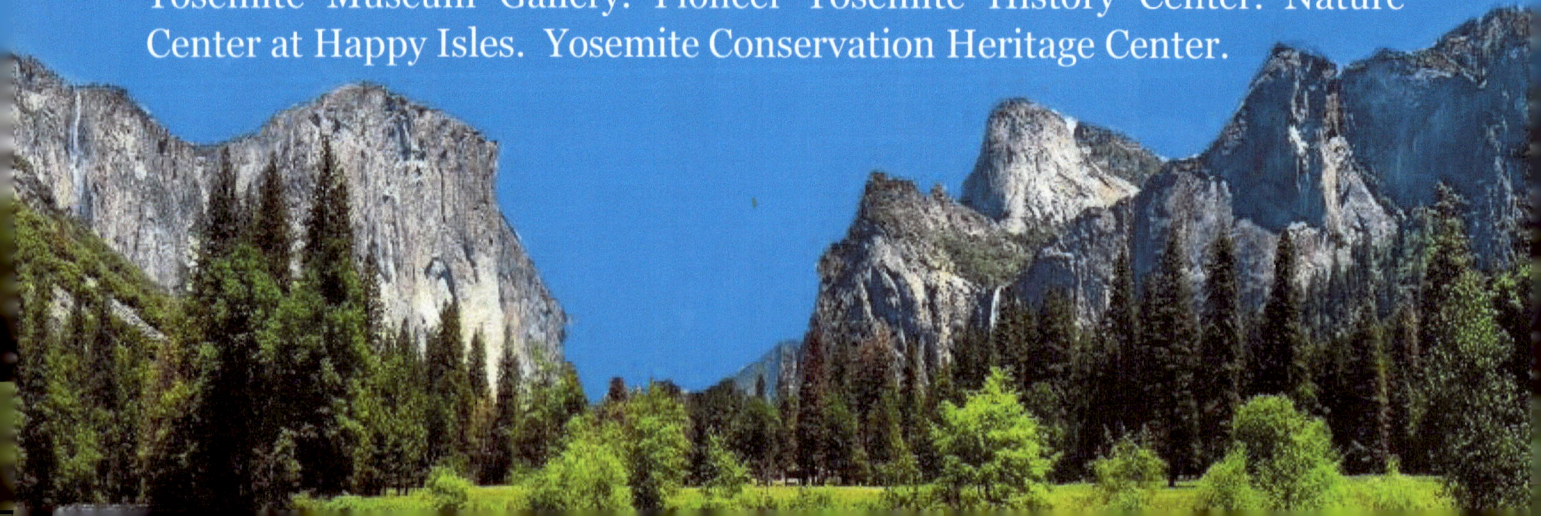

Some of the activities and sights to see in Yosemite are free. Some do require fees, check before going. There are many ways to view the park. You can walk, hike, ride a bike or drive and see many of the sights. The park also has camping and swimming areas. Pets are welcomed only in select places throughout Yosemite, check the rules before you go.

We couldn't list everything the park has to offer for sights to see. But the main areas we listed will take you to many more of the sights not listed and many more sightseeing opportunities.

The best times to visit Yosemite is May to September, when the park is accessible. It's important to know that at certain times of the year, the roads may be closed due to snow.

Always check ahead of time, before planning your trip.

Thanks.

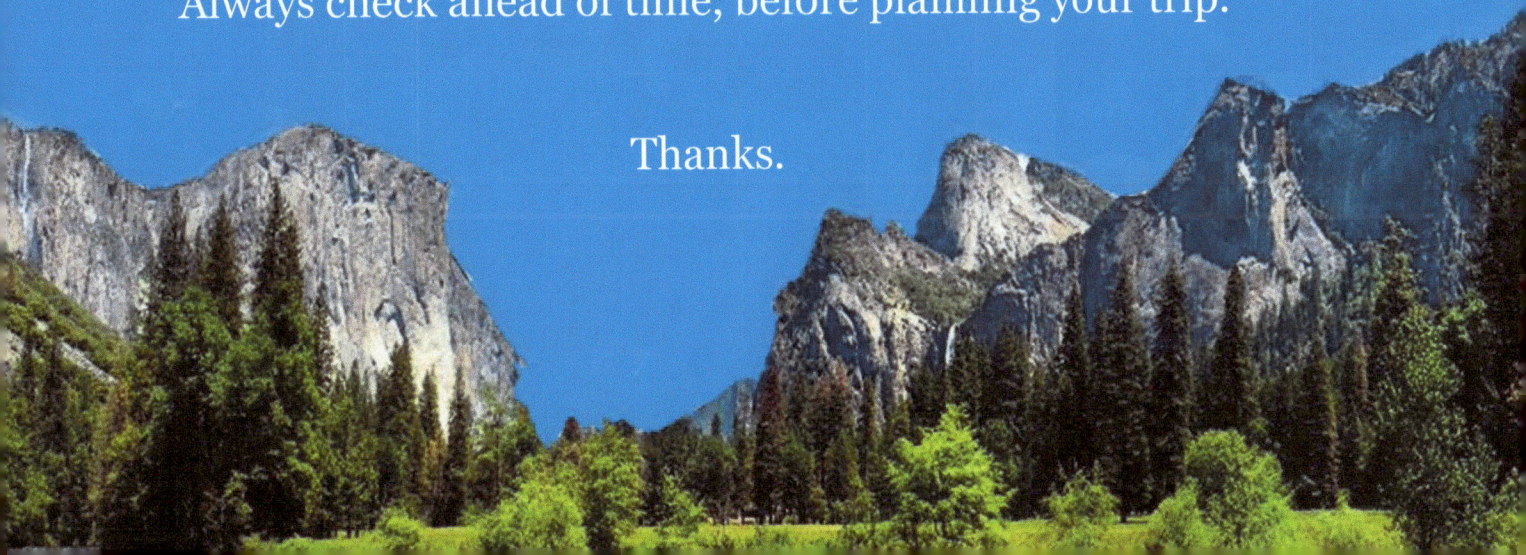

Author Page

Billy Grinslott & Kinsey Marie Books

ISBN – 9781960612908

Thanks

www.ingramcontent.com/pod-product-compliance
Lightning Source LLC
Chambersburg PA
CBHW060822270326
41931CB00002B/56